Internet
Scavenger Hunts
Science

Instant Reproducibles for 20 Exciting Internet Explorations
That Enrich Learning and Get Kids Web-Savvy

by Maria L. Chang

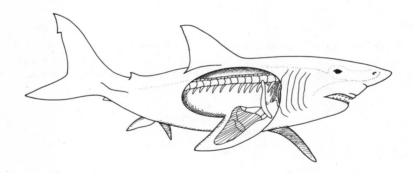

SCHOLASTIC
PROFESSIONAL BOOKS

New York • Toronto • London • Auckland • Sydney • Mexico City
New Delhi • Hong Kong • Buenos Aires

For Jason, Zachary, and Jeremy

Cover design by **Norma Ortiz**
Interior design by **Holly Grundon**
Illustrations by **Ivy Rutzky**

Cover Images: "Amusement Park Physics" Web page reproduced courtesy of Annenberg/CPB, a partnership between the Annenberg Foundation and the Corporation for Public Broadcasting to advance excellent teaching. "Sharks" Web page reproduced courtesy of National Parks Conservations Association (www.eparks.org).

ISBN 0-439-13846-9
Copyright © 2002 by Maria L. Chang
All rights reserved.
Printed in the U.S.A.

4 5 6 7 8 9 10   40   08 07 06 05 04 03

Contents

Introduction

In the last few years, the Internet has grown to become such an important resource for almost everyone that it's hard to imagine what life was like before it existed. As a teacher, you may use the Internet to search for lesson plans and activities, communicate with other teachers and classrooms from around the country, and get advice from professional developers.

Students are getting into the act, too. Just look at these facts about Internet usage in U.S. public schools from Quality Education Data (2001):

- **97 percent of America's public schools are connected to the Internet**

- **84 percent of all public school classrooms are connected to the Internet**

- **74 percent of students spend one hour or more per week hands-on at school with the Internet**

- **96 percent of students who use the Internet weekly use it for research**

The Internet is such an incredibly rich resource, it's tempting to send students to the computer to do research on their own. But sitting a student in front of the Internet is much like leaving a student in the library and expecting him to find out about tectonic plates. Just as it's necessary for students to learn library research skills, it's also important to teach them how to do research on the Internet. That's where this book comes in.

Using This Book

Inside, you'll find more than 50 reproducible pages of Internet scavenger hunts on 20 high-interest science topics that you teach. Scavenger hunts offer a quick and easy way to give your students practice in doing research on the Internet.

Some of the activity sheets send students on a fact-finding mission to look for specific information, such as names of 10 dinosaurs that lived during the Jurassic Period, or the brain weight of a humpback whale, chimpanzee, alligator, and other animals. Other activities go one step further and require students to do something with the information they find. For example, after gathering information about triglobites (cave dwellers), students write a report describing a newly discovered species. Still others require more critical thinking —students figure out how a shark's body is especially adapted for hunting prey, or draw an imaginary animal that is adapted to a biome that they created.

Use these self-guided scavenger hunts to introduce students to a new topic, supplement your lesson plan, or assign them as independent work.

Accessing the Web Sites

R eady to get students started on their Internet scavenger hunts? Send them to our Web site at:

http://www.scholastic.com/profbooks/easyinternet/index.htm

This address appears at the top of each reproducible activity page. When students reach this site, have them click on the book thumbnail of *Internet Scavenger Hunts: Science*. This will take them directly to a page that lists all the links for the activities. You may want to bookmark this site or add it to your favorites. To access the Web sites needed to complete each activity, have students click on the links under the activity name.

Even though we regularly update the links on our Web site, you may still want to check the links yourself before using them in your classroom. This way, you can make sure that the material on the site is appropriate for your students, and familiarize yourself with the content so you can help students as needed.

TIPS
for a
SUCCESSFUL HUNT

The activities in this book are designed so students can work independently, either individually or in small groups. To help students get the most out of their time online, share with them these helpful tips before they embark on their Internet scavenger hunts:

1. Read the activity sheet carefully before going to the computer. This way, students will know ahead of time what kind of information they need to find. You may want to go over the worksheet as a class to discuss any questions students may have.

2. Browse through the Web site for relevant information. Tell students that they don't have to read everything on the site. They can just skim through until they find the information they need. Have them refer back to their worksheets regularly so they know what to look for next.

3. Explore the various links on the page to get more information. On some Web sites, certain pictures or words within the text may be highlighted or underlined. Clicking on these links usually opens another page that gives more in-depth information. (Note: As much as possible, we've tried to avoid Web sites with advertisements. However, some very useful sites do have them. Caution students against clicking on any ads that may appear on a page.)

4. Use the commands Find or Find Again under the Edit toolbar to help search for a particular word on the Web page. For example, if students are looking for the definition of "axon," they could quickly look for the word on the Web page by using the command Find.

TIPS *for the* ONE-COMPUTER CLASSROOM

You say you only have one computer in your classroom? With a few management tips, your class can still enjoy doing the activities in this book:

1. Hook up your computer to a video monitor or a projector so that the class can browse the Web together. Invite students to participate by taking turns clicking on the hyperlinks or reading the information.

2. You can save Web pages as viewable documents. Or, you can print out a Web site beforehand and hand out photocopies to students. Just make sure that you print out all the relevant pages and links that your students need to complete their activity pages.

3. If you have other computers in your classroom that aren't hooked up to the Internet, use an offline software such as Web Whacker to capture and download all the pages of a Web site.

4. Assign small groups of students to work together on the computer for about 15 to 20 minutes in rotation. Give the rest of the class other related activities to do while waiting their turn on the computer.

5. If students have access to the Internet at home, consider assigning the pages as homework. You can get them started on Step 1 and have them finish their work at home.

Name: _____ Date: _____

Insects

The Good, the Bad. . . the Bugs

Insects are not all that creepy. Some are very helpful to humans, while others are just pests. Explore the links at the above Web site to find out which bugs are "good" and which are "bad." Pick two of each kind and print their pictures to paste in the spaces below. Write their names and reasons why you think these bugs are good or bad.

☐ Good Bug
☐ Bad Bug

Name: _____

What It Does: _____

_____

☐ Good Bug
☐ Bad Bug

Name: _____

What It Does: _____

_____

☐ Good Bug
☐ Bad Bug

Name: _____

What It Does: _____

_____

☐ Good Bug
☐ Bad Bug

Name: _____

What It Does: _____

_____

Name: _____ Date: _____

GO TO: http://www.scholastic.com/profbooks/easyinternet/index.htm

Insects

Ultimate Survivors

Cockroaches have been around for more than 250 million years. How have these bugs managed to survive for so long? Click on the links at the above Web site to find out how the cockroach's anatomy helps it survive. Below, write how each of the following body parts helps the cockroach live through another day.

Eyes	
Antennae	
Brain	
Legs	
Cerci	
Fat body	
Reproductive system	

Name: _____   Date: _____

Insects

A Pest for a Pet

A dog needs to be walked, a cat fed, and a bird cleaned up
after. But what do you need to care for a cockroach?
Click on the links at the above Web site to find
out. Then fill in the chart below to see what
this pest . . . er, pet . . . needs.

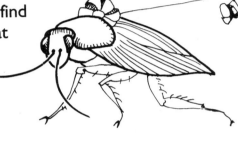

1.	**Habitat**	
2.	**Food**	
3.	**Water**	
4.	**Care**	
5.	**What else does it need?**	

Name: _____ Date: _____

GO TO: http://www.scholastic.com/profbooks/easyinternet/index.htm

Sharks

Shark or Dolphin?

Splashing in the sun-warmed ocean, you suddenly spot a fin slice the water near you. Uh-oh! Is that a ferocious shark or a friendly dolphin? Click on the links at the above Web site to learn the difference between these marine animals. Use the Venn diagram below to list the characteristics of each animal in the appropriate circle. Write the characteristics both animals have in common in the overlapping area.

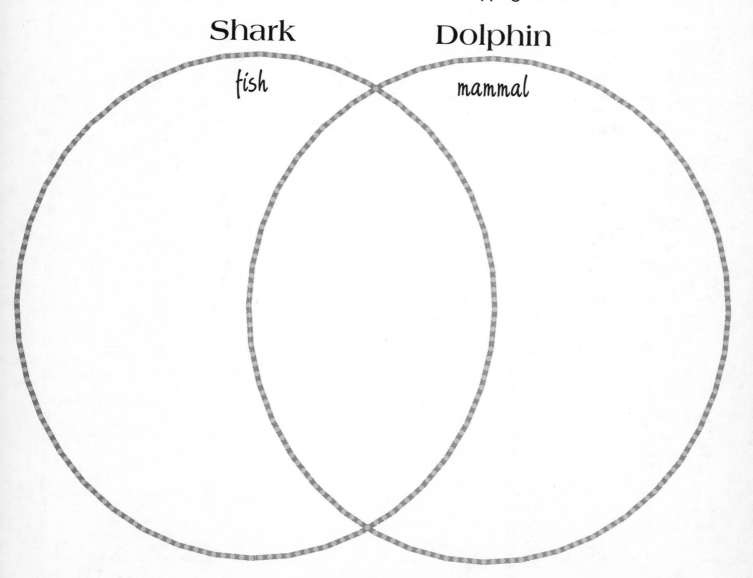

Shark   Dolphin

fish   mammal

Name: _____

GO TO: http://www.scholastic.com/profbooks/easyinternet/index.htm

Sharks **Master Hunter**

The shark is one of the best hunters in the ocean, thanks to its well-designed body. Find out how the shark's body helps it catch its prey by visiting the links at the above Web site. In the boxes below, write how each body part helps the shark be a master hunter.

nostrils

ampullae of Lorenzini

eyes

teeth

gills

fins

cartilage

skin

Name: _____ Date: _____

GO TO: http://www.scholastic.com/profbooks/easyinternet/index.htm

Sharks

Shark Fact or Fiction

How much do you really know about sharks? Click on the links at the above Web site to read more about these fearsome creatures. Figure out which of the following statements are fact or fiction. Circle the letter under the correct heading. Then write the letter above the corresponding number at the bottom of the page to answer the Trivia Tracker.

Fact	Fiction		
E	P	1.	During its lifetime a shark can grow thousands and thousands of new teeth.
F	A	2.	The great white shark is the biggest species of shark.
G	L	3.	The first sharks appeared soon after dinosaurs became extinct.
D	O	4.	Humans attack sharks more often than sharks attack humans.
T	C	5.	Most shark species are bigger than humans.
R	S	6.	Like all fish, sharks have a bony skeleton.
I	A	7.	Sharks can sense electromagnetic fields underwater to help them find food.
U	E	8.	Each year, sharks kill about 100 people.
T	B	9.	There are more than 350 species of sharks.
H	N	10.	Sharks swim only in the salty oceans.

Trivia Tracker

A shark's sandpaper-like skin is made up of "tiny teeth" called

__ __ __ __ __ __   __ __ __ __ __ __ __ __ __
4   1   10   9   2   3   4   8   10   9   7   5   3   1   6

Name: _____ Date: _____

Dinosaurs

When Did Dinosaurs Roam the Earth?

Remember the scary Tyrannosaurus rex in the movie *Jurassic Park*? What's scarier is that the T. rex wasn't alive during the Jurassic Period—it lived during the Cretaceous Period. Browse the links at the above Web site and list up to 10 dinosaur species that lived in each of the time periods below.

	Triassic Period (248 to 206 million years ago)	**Jurassic Period** (206 to 144 million years ago)	**Cretaceous Period** (144 to 65 million years ago)
1.			
2.			
3.			
4.			
5.			
6.			
7.			
8.			
9.			
10.			

Name: _____ Date: _____

GO TO: http://www.scholastic.com/profbooks/easyinternet/index.htm

Dinosaurs

What's in a Dino Name?

A newly discovered dinosaur species may be named after a person or the place in which it was discovered. But most dino names come from Greek or Latin root words that describe the dinosaur's physical characteristics or likely behavior. Click on the links at the above Web site to define the root words below.

1. acantho _____
2. bellu _____
3. cephalo _____
4. don or dont _____
5. hadro _____

6. micro _____
7. ops _____
8. pedi _____
9. tri _____
10. venator _____

What do these dinosaur names mean?

11. compsognathus _____

12. triceratops _____

13. velociraptor _____

14. deinonychus _____

15. tyrannosaurus rex _____

Name: _____ Date: _____

GO TO: http://www.scholastic.com/profbooks/easyinternet/index.htm

Dinosaurs

Gone the Way of the Dinosaurs

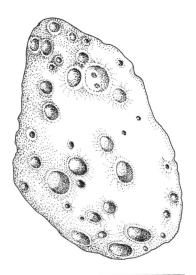

Dinosaurs roamed the Earth for nearly 200 million years, then suddenly they were gone! What killed off the dinosaurs? Read scientists' different theories by visiting the links at the above Web site. Compare the theories in the chart below, writing whether or not you think each theory is valid and why.

Theory	What It Says	What Do You Think?
A giant asteroid hit the Earth		
Volcanic activity increased		
A supernova exploded nearby		
Diseases spread among the dinosaurs		
Other theory? _____		

Name: _____ Date: _____

GO TO: http://www.scholastic.com/profbooks/easyinternet/index.htm

Nervous System & the Brain

Control Center

Inside our body is a highly complex network called the nervous system that keeps track of what goes on in the outside world and controls how we react to it. Read more about the nervous system and its components by clicking on the links at the above Web site. Then match the words in the left column with the correct definitions at the right.

Trivia Tracker

What are the two halves of the brain called?

_____

_____ 1. nervous system

_____ 2. neuron

_____ 3. neurotransmitters

_____ 4. spinal cord

_____ 5. vertebrae

_____ 6. somatic nervous system

_____ 7. autonomic nervous system

_____ 8. synapse

_____ 9. dendrite

_____ 10. axon

A. controls skeletal muscles and voluntary movement

B. long bundle of nerves that runs down your back

C. nerve cell extension that takes information away from the cell

D. small gap that separates two nerve cells

E. nerve cell

F. nerve cell extension that brings information to the cell

G. body system made up of the brain, spinal cord, and nerves

H. bones that protect the spinal cord

I. controls smooth muscles of internal organs and glands

J. chemicals that carry signals between nerve cells

Name: _____ Date: _____

GO TO: http://www.scholastic.com/profbooks/easyinternet/index.htm

Nervous System & the Brain
The Brain Knows

Thinking, walking, eating, breathing . . . all of these actions are controlled by your brain. But which part of your brain controls what actions? Click on the links at the above Web site to find out. Then match each activity below to the part of the brain that helps you do it. Write the letter of the correct brain part in the blank.

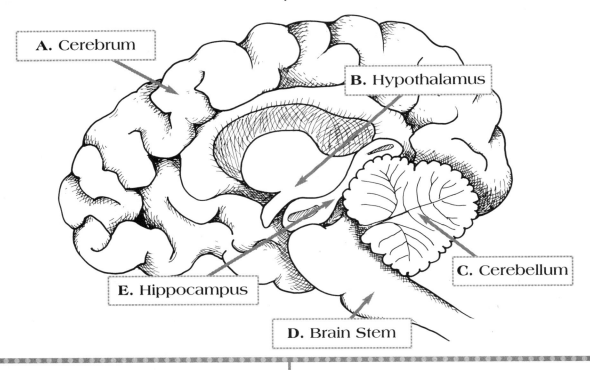

A. Cerebrum

B. Hypothalamus

C. Cerebellum

E. Hippocampus

D. Brain Stem

1. _____ Calculating the amount of money in your pocket

2. _____ Feeling feverish from the heat

3. _____ Riding a bicycle to school

4. _____ Remembering to do your homework

5. _____ Shivering in the cold rain

6. _____ Thinking about what you had for dinner last night

7. _____ Reading the latest comic book

8. _____ Digesting the pizza you just ate

9. _____ Snapping your fingers in time to music

10. _____ Your heart beating faster as you run

Name: _____ Date: _____

GO TO: http://www.scholastic.com/profbooks/easyinternet/index.htm

Nervous System & the Brain

Weigh Those Brains

The adult human brain weighs about 1,300 grams or 3 pounds. How do other animals' brains compare? Click on the links at the above Web site to find out. Then list animals' brain weights in the chart below. Don't forget to include the unit of measurement.

Trivia Tracker

How much did a stegosaurus's brain weigh?

_____

Animal	Brain Weight
Adult Human	1,300 grams
Elephant	
Owl	
Rhesus Monkey	
Humpback Whale	
Chimpanzee	
Rat	
Alligator	
Squirrel	
Tiger	

Think About It!

1. Which of the animal brains at left weighs the most?

_____

2. Which of the animals at left would you say weighs the most?

_____

3. Do you think there's a relationship between an animal's size and its brain size?

What is it? _____

_____

4. Do you think there's a relationship between an animal's brain size and its intelligence? Why or why not?

_____

_____

Name: _____ Date: _____

GO TO: http://www.scholastic.com/profbooks/easyinternet/index.htm

Sleep

Sleepy Time

Sleep is probably the most underrated human activity, yet without it we'd die. Visit the links at the above Web site to learn more about this all-important function, then answer the questions below.

Trivia Tracker

About what fraction of our lives is spent sleeping?

_____

1. How many stages of sleep are there? _____

2. In which stages are you most likely to awaken? _____

3. In which stage do you dream? _____

4. Which stages are considered "deep sleep"? _____

5. What does REM stand for? Why is it called that? _____

   _____

6. About what percentage of the sleep cycle do
   infants spend on REM? How about adults? _____

7. What happens to your body during the first stage of sleep? _____

   _____

8. About how many times in one night does a person
   cycle through the different stages of sleep? _____

9. Which activity can your body go without
   for a longer time—sleeping or eating? _____

10. How does sleep affect your brain? _____

Name: _____   Date: _____

GO TO: http://www.scholastic.com/profbooks/easyinternet/index.htm

Sleep

Selling Sleep

Sleep is probably the most important activity we do all day, yet many people feel it's just a waste of time. Find out why we need sleep by exploring the links at the above Web site. Below, list five reasons we need sleep and five tips on how to get a good night's sleep. Using your lists for reference, write a 5-minute "infomercial" at the back of this page to convince kids that sleep is essential.

Reasons We Need Sleep

1.

2.

3.

4.

5.

Tips on How to Get a Good Night's Sleep

1.

2.

3.

4.

5.

Name: _____ Date: _____

GO TO: http://www.scholastic.com/profbooks/easyinternet/index.htm

Plants
Plant Parts

There are more than 400,000 species of plants in the world, and they all come in different shapes and sizes. Whatever they look like, most plants have the same parts. Click on the links at the above Web site to learn more about these green citizens of the Earth. Then list three facts about each plant part below.

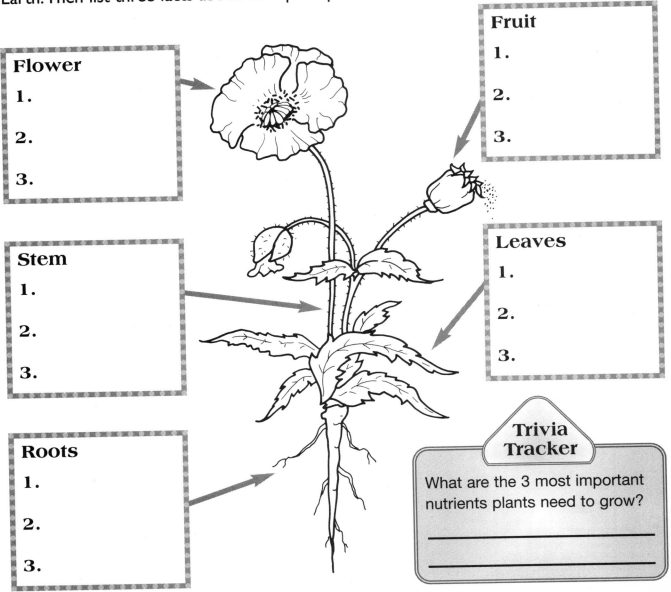

Fruit
1.
2.
3.

Flower
1.
2.
3.

Stem
1.
2.
3.

Leaves
1.
2.
3.

Roots
1.
2.
3.

Trivia Tracker

What are the 3 most important nutrients plants need to grow?

_____

_____

GO TO: http://www.scholastic.com/profbooks/easyinternet/index.htm

Plants

Food Factory Crossword

Click on the links at the above Web site to solve the crossword puzzle.

Across

1. Pores on a leaf's surface that take in carbon dioxide
5. Word that means "making things with light"
8. Liquid that plants need to make sugar
9. Green substance in leaves that captures the sun's light energy
12. Type of sugar that plants make

Down

2. Waste product given off by leaves after making sugar
3. Kind of energy that leaves convert the sun's light energy into

4. Tiny tubes in leaves that carry water and minerals
6. Complex carbohydrate made by leaves from sugar
7. Main source of energy for all living things
10. A plant's food factories
11. Element that plants get from water to make food

Name: _____ Date: _____

GO TO: http://www.scholastic.com/profbooks/easyinternet/index.htm

Plants

Seeds on the Move

For new plants to grow, seeds have to reach good growing places where they can get enough water, nutrients, and sunlight. Browse the links at the above Web site to find out how seeds get to good growing places. Pick a seed for each travel method below and draw each one. Explain how the seed's structure helps it reach its destination.

By Wind

By Water

By Animal

GO TO: http://www.scholastic.com/profbooks/easyinternet/index.htm

Plants
Meet the Meat-Eaters

Meat-eating or carnivorous plants don't get enough nutrients from the soil they grow in. Instead, they eat insects or other small animals to survive. How do these plants that are rooted to the ground catch fast-moving bugs? Check out the links at the above Web site to find out. Then fill out the chart below.

Carnivorous Plant	Where Does It Grow?	How Does It Trap Food?	What Kind of Prey Does It Eat?
Venus fly trap (Dionaea)			
Pitcher plant (Nepenthes or Sarracenia)			
Sundew plant (Drosera)			
Bladderwort (Utricularia)			

Name: _____ Date: _____

GO TO: http://www.scholastic.com/profbooks/easyinternet/index.htm

Biomes
Around the World

Is it always hot and dry where you live? Or do you experience spring, summer, fall, and winter? Different parts of the world have different climates. The community of plants and animals that live in a specific climate is called a *biome*. Explore different biomes at the links at the above Web site. Color in the world map below to show the location of each biome. Don't forget to color in the map key as well.

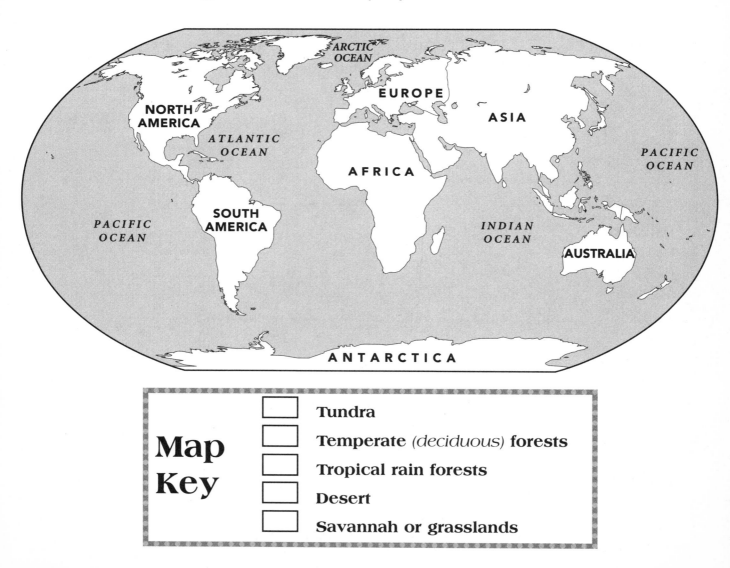

Map Key

- [ ] **Tundra**
- [ ] **Temperate** (*deciduous*) **forests**
- [ ] **Tropical rain forests**
- [ ] **Desert**
- [ ] **Savannah or grasslands**

Name: _____ Date: _____

Biomes
Comparing Biomes

How are the biomes different from one another? Click on the links at the above Web site to find out. Then fill in the chart below to describe characteristics of each biome and list the different plants and animals that live in each one.

Biome	What is it like?	What plants and animals live there?
Tundra		
Desert		
Tropical Rain Forest		
Temperate Forest		
Savannah		

Name: _____ Date: _____

GO TO: http://www.scholastic.com/profbooks/easyinternet/index.htm

Biomes
Invent an Animal

Can you imagine an elephant living in the cold Arctic? Or a polar bear in the hot desert? Each animal has special adaptations that help it survive in the biome in which it lives. Learn more from the links at the above Web site. Then make up and describe your own biome. Think about what kind of animal could survive in it. Draw a picture of your animal in the box and explain how it is adapted to your biome.

My Biome
Describe your biome here. What is the climate like? What kind of shelter and food is available?

_____

_____

_____

_____

My Animal

Name: _____ Date: _____

GO TO: http://www.scholastic.com/profbooks/easyinternet/index.htm

Oceans
Dive Into the Deep

Looking at the ocean's flat surface, it's hard to believe that the tallest mountains and the deepest valleys lie underneath. Scientists divide the ocean into zones, from its surface to its deepest depths. Click on the links at the above Web site to learn more. Label the drawing with the names and depths of each zone. Then draw an animal that lives in each zone. Color your drawings and the different zones.

GO TO: http://www.scholastic.com/profbooks/easyinternet/index.htm

Oceans

Facts About the Oceans

The oceans cover more than 70 percent of the Earth's surface. But what exactly do you know about them? Click on the links at the above Web site to read more about the world's four oceans. Then list five facts about each one below, including its area and depth.

Pacific Ocean

1.

2.

3.

4.

5.

Indian Ocean

1.

2.

3.

4.

5.

Atlantic Ocean

1.

2.

3.

4.

5.

Arctic Ocean

1.

2.

3.

4.

5.

Name: _____ Date: _____

GO TO: http://www.scholastic.com/profbooks/easyinternet/index.htm

Coral Reefs

Colorful Corals

Do the words "coral reef" conjure images of tropical islands, clear blue water, and colorful underwater formations? Explore coral reefs by clicking on the links at the above Web site. Then use the word bank to fill in the blanks below.

Trivia Tracker

What land ecosystem is a coral reef often compared to?

_____

Word Bank
atoll
Australia
calcium carbonate
fringing reefs
humans
polyps
predators
sea anemones
tropical
zooxanthellae

1. Corals are made up of tiny animals called _____.

2. Coral reefs are found in warm _____ oceans near the equator.

3. The substance that makes coral hard is _____.

4. An _____ is a type of reef that surrounds a central lagoon.

5. The world's largest reef, the Great Barrier Reef, is located in _____.

6. _____ are animals with stinging tentacles that live in coral reefs with clownfish for companions.

7. _____ are algae that have a symbiotic relationship with coral polyps.

8. Coral reefs that grow in shallow water and border the coast are called _____.

9. Nooks and crannies in coral reefs offer places for tiny fish to hide from their _____.

10. The biggest threat to corals are _____.

Name: _____ Date: _____

GO TO: http://www.scholastic.com/profbooks/easyinternet/index.htm

Coral Reefs

Save the Corals

Around the world, coral reefs are in danger of disappearing. Click on the links at the above Web site to find out why. List five of the greatest threats to corals below, as well as five suggestions on how we can help save them. Then design a poster urging people to save these underwater wonders.

Threats to coral reefs

1.

2.

3.

4.

5.

What we can do to help

1.

2.

3.

4.

5.

Name: _____ Date: _____

GO TO: http://www.scholastic.com/profbooks/easyinternet/index.htm

Caves

How Caves Form

Caves take thousands of years to form, and most of them start out the same way. Click on the links at the above Web site to find out about cave formation. Then caption the drawing below, explaining in detail what's happening in the picture and how a cave forms.

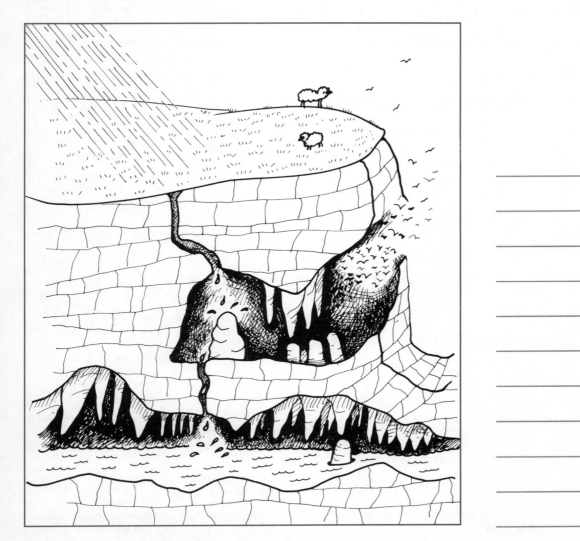

_____

_____

_____

_____

_____

_____

_____

_____

_____

_____

Name: _____ Date: _____

Caves
Underground Wonders

Click on the links at the above Web site to see and read about unusual cave formations. Read each description below and write the word it describes in the spaces, one letter per space. Then unscramble the letters inside the circles to answer the Trivia Tracker.

1. Thin, hollow tube that forms when water drips from the cave ceiling through its center

    Ⓞ — — —   Ⓞ — — —

2. Mineral deposit that hangs from a cave ceiling

    — — — — — — — Ⓞ — Ⓞ

3. Mineral deposit that builds up from the cave floor

    — — — — — Ⓞ — — Ⓞ —

4. Structure that goes all the way from the cave's ceiling to the floor

    — Ⓞ — — — —

5. Irregular clusters of calcium carbonate that grows on cave walls or floor

    — — Ⓞ — — — —

6. Formations in slanted cave ceilings that look like curtains

    — — — — Ⓞ — — —

7. Feature that forms when water flows over a wall or floor, leaving a film of calcium carbonate

    — Ⓞ — — — Ⓞ — —

8. Layer of calcite that forms around a grain of sand

    — — — — — — — — Ⓞ —

Trivia Tracker What do you call a person who studies caves?

Name: _____ Date: _____

GO TO: http://www.scholastic.com/profbooks/easyinternet/index.htm

Caves

Creatures of the Dark

Some animals, like bats or owls, hang out in caves for part of their lives. But there are animals that live out their whole lives inside caves. These are called *triglobites*. Check out the links at the above Web site to learn more about these fascinating creatures and fill in the graphic organizer below.

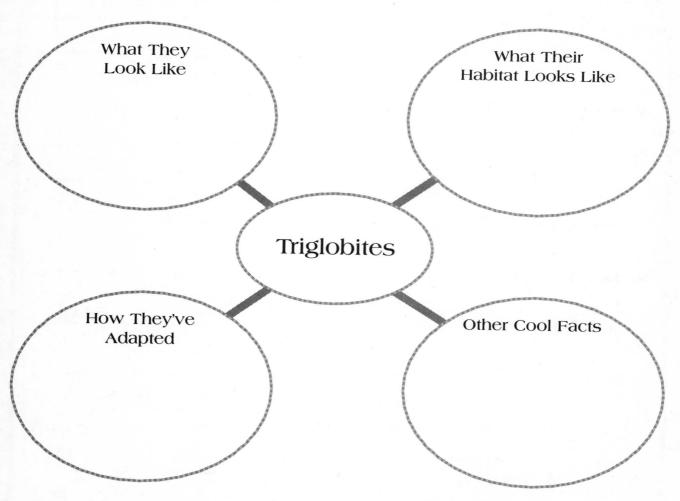

What They
Look Like

What Their
Habitat Looks Like

Triglobites

How They've
Adapted

Other Cool Facts

Pretend you're a scientist who has just discovered a new species of triglobite. Write about your discovery at the back of this page, describing the creature you've found. Include the facts you've listed above in your report.

Name: _____ Date: _____

Plate Tectonics

The Moving Earth

Believe it or not, the ground that you're standing on is always on the move. The theory of plate tectonics says that the Earth's outermost layer is broken into huge slabs called *plates* that are always moving in different directions at different speeds. Click on the links at the above Web site to learn more about plate tectonics. Then answer the questions below.

1. When was the theory of plate tectonics developed? _____

2. Who first proposed that the continents were moving? _____

3. Name one proof used to support this theory. _____

   _____

4. What is the lithosphere? _____

5. How many major (very large) plates make up the Earth's crust? _____

6. About how fast do the plates move each year? _____

7. What are three types of plate boundaries? _____

8. What kind of boundary forms tall mountain ranges? _____

9. What kind of boundary makes up the San Andreas Fault? _____

10. What two natural disasters are commonly associated with the movement of plates?

   _____

Name: _____ Date: _____

GO TO: http://www.scholastic.com/profbooks/easyinternet/index.htm

Plate Tectonics

Crossing Boundaries

The gigantic plates the make up the Earth's crust fit together like a jigsaw puzzle. The plates' boundaries move against each other in different ways. Explore the links at the above Web site to learn more about different boundaries. Then draw each one and caption your drawing with an explanation of how it works.

Convergent Boundary

Divergent Boundary

Transform Boundary

Name: _____ Date: _____

GO TO: http://www.scholastic.com/profbooks/easyinternet/index.htm

Earthquakes

Mapping Earth's Shakes

Many earthquakes happen when the earth's plates move against each other. Research the links at the above Web site to find out where some of the biggest earthquakes in the last century occurred. List the places, then plot them on the map below. You may want to refer to another world map to see the countries' names.

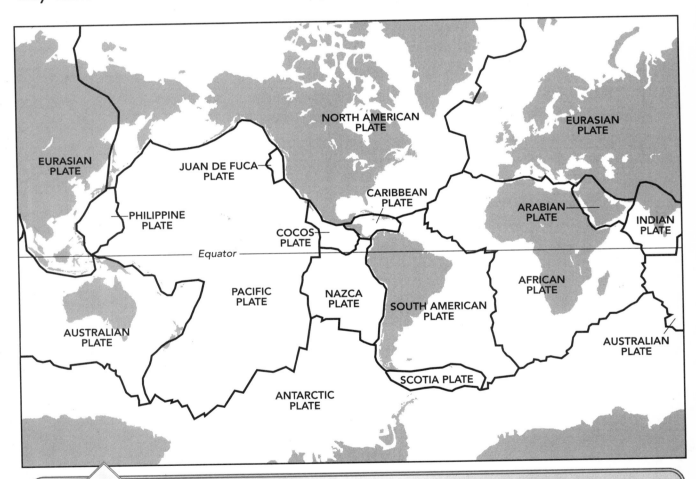

Think About It | What do you notice about where many of the earthquakes occur?

_____

Name: _____ Date: _____

GO TO: http://www.scholastic.com/profbooks/easyinternet/index.htm

Earthquakes

Tremor Terminology

All the words and phrases used to describe earthquakes is enough to rattle the brain. Check out the links at the above Web site to familiarize yourself with earthquake terminology. Then match the words or phrases in the left column with the correct definitions at the right.

Trivia Tracker

When and where was the earliest recorded earthquake?

_____

_____ 1. focus

_____ 2. epicenter

_____ 3. surface waves

_____ 4. body waves

_____ 5. Richter scale

_____ 6. fault

_____ 7. subduction zone

_____ 8. magnitude

_____ 9. seismograph

_____ 10. intensity

A. fracture between two slabs of rock on the Earth's crust

B. a measure of an earthquake's strength based on how things look after a quake

C. occurs when one plate rides atop another plate and pushes it down into the mantle

D. place on the Earth's surface directly above the focus

E. seismic vibrations that pass through the Earth's interior

F. place inside the Earth where an earthquake originates

G. mathematical scale used to measure the magnitude of earthquakes

H. instrument used to detect, record, and measure earthquakes

I. seismic vibrations that cause most of the damage from earthquakes

J. a measure of an earthquake's strength based on the amplitude of seismic waves

Name: _____ Date: _____

GO TO: http://www.scholastic.com/profbooks/easyinternet/index.htm

Earthquakes

Earthquakes Do's and Don't's

When the ground starts to shake and windows rattle, people can't help but panic. So what are you supposed to do—and not do—during an earthquake? Visit the links at the above Web site to find out. Then list the do's and don't's of earthquake safety.

	Do's	Don't's
1.		
2.		
3.		
4.		
5.		
6.		
7.		
8.		
9.		
10.		

Name: _____ Date: _____

GO TO: http://www.scholastic.com/profbooks/easyinternet/index.htm

Earthquakes

Tsunami Trivia

Sometimes, an earthquake can trigger a *tsunami*, or giant wave, that washes over coastal areas. Learn more about tsunamis by clicking on the links at the above Web site. Then answer the questions below.

1. What's the difference between a tsunami and a tidal wave? _____

_____

2. From what language did the word "tsunami" originate? _____

3. What is considered the tsunami capital of the United States? _____

4. Name three causes of tsunamis. _____

_____

5. What caused the tsunami that struck the Hawaiian islands in April of 1946? _____

_____

6. Which ocean is most likely to have tsunamis? Why? _____

_____

7. How fast do tsunamis travel in the ocean? _____

8. About how long would it take a tsunami to cross the Pacific Ocean? _____

9. Up to how high can tsunamis reach? _____

10. Where should people who are at risk go when a tsunami is coming? _____

Name: _____ Date: _____

GO TO: http://www.scholastic.com/profbooks/easyinternet/index.htm

Thunderstorms

Thunder and Lightning

Powerful storms pummel the Earth's surface more frequently than we imagine. Learn more about thunderstorms from the links at the above Web site. Then read the statements below. The underlined words are false. Rewrite them to make the sentences true.

1. About 1,000 thunderstorms occur on the Earth's surface at any given time.

2. Every day, up to 50,000 thunderstorms rage across the United States.

3. Lightning strikes the Earth about 100 times per minute.

4. Thunderstorms begin to develop when cold air near the Earth's surface rises above higher, warmer air.

5. A typical thunderstorm lasts about 5 minutes.

6. To figure out how many miles away lightning is, count the number of minutes between lightning and thunder and divide it by 10.

7. Severe thunderstorms can produce hurricanes, whirling columns of air that touch down from a thunderstorm cloud.

8. Hailstones produced by thunderstorms range in size from as small as an egg to as big as a basketball.

9. Downbursts are strong winds that rise into a thunderstorm cloud.

10. Heat released when water vapor turns to liquid cloud particles weakens a thunderstorm and causes it to end.

Name: _____ Date: _____

GO TO: http://www.scholastic.com/profbooks/easyinternet/index.htm

Thunderstorms
Wild Weather

Severe thunderstorms wreak havoc in more ways than one. Find out how by clicking on the links at the above Web site. Name three "side effects" of thunderstorms, then list three facts about them, including how they form and what kind of damage they can do.

```
                    ┌─────────────────────┐
                    │   Thunderstorms     │
                    └─────────────────────┘
     ┌───────────────┐  ┌───────────────┐  ┌───────────────┐
     │               │  │               │  │               │
     │               │  │               │  │               │
     │               │  │               │  │               │
     └───────────────┘  └───────────────┘  └───────────────┘
```

1. _____   1. _____   1. _____

  _____   _____   _____

2. _____   2. _____   2. _____

  _____   _____   _____

3. _____   3. _____   3. _____

  _____   _____   _____

Name: _____ Date: _____

Thunderstorms

How Lightning Strikes

You can always tell a thunderstorm is near by the bolts of lightning that zigzag across the sky. Click on the links at the above Web site to find out what makes lightning. Add (+) and (-) to the drawing below to show where these electrical charges can be found during a thunderstorm. Then cut out the labels below and paste them next to the appropriate spots to explain what's happening in the picture.

As thunderstorm clouds build up, their upper layers become positively charged, while the clouds' lower layers become negatively charged.

As the clouds pass over the ground, they induce a positive charge on the ground.

As charges build up in the clouds and on the ground, they overcome air's natural resistance to the flow of electricity. Positive charges from the ground flow up to meet the negative charges coming down from the clouds. Lightning!

GO TO: http://www.scholastic.com/profbooks/easyinternet/index.htm

The Sun

Solar Crossword

Bet you didn't know there were a lot of words related to the sun. Read about the sun by browsing through the links at the above Web site. Then use what you've learned to solve the crossword puzzle below.

Across

2. The sun's outer visible layer

3. The family of planets, moons, asteroids, and comets around the sun

8. Process that is the source of the sun's energy

10. Gas that makes up most of the sun

11. Type of star that the sun will turn into when it swells up and swallows the Earth

12. Process that carries solar energy from the sun's center to its surface

14. Charged particles emitted by the sun into space

15. Bright filament of hot gas that erupts from the corona

5. Dark, cooler area on the sun's surface

6. Second-most abundant gas in the sun

7. Huge cloud of gas that erupts from the corona

9. Center of the sun where solar energy is produced

13. Outermost layer of the sun that's visible only during an eclipse

Down

1. Layer above the photosphere

4. What the sun really is

Name: _____ Date: _____

GO TO: http://www.scholastic.com/profbooks/easyinternet/index.htm

The Sun

By the Numbers

The sun is so huge that most numbers used to describe it are equally big. Check out the links at the above Web site to see some statistics about our closest star. Then fill in the blanks below with the correct numbers. (You may round off some of the numbers.)

1. The sun is _____ miles away from the Earth.

2. The sun is about _____ billion years old.

3. Scientists think the sun will be around for another _____ billion years.

4. The sun is about _____ kilometers in diameter.

5. It takes about _____ days for the sun to rotate near its equator.

6. Near the poles, the sun takes about _____ days to make a complete rotation.

7. The temperature on the sun's surface is about _____ degrees Kelvin.

8. At the core, its temperature is about _____ degrees Kelvin.

9. Every _____ years, the sun's activity increases.

10. It takes about _____ minutes for the sun's light to reach the Earth.

Trivia Tracker   If you could drive to the sun in a car at about 60 miles per hour, how long would it take you to get there?

_____

Name: _____   Date: _____

GO TO: http://www.scholastic.com/profbooks/easyinternet/index.htm

Eclipses

Which Eclipse Is That Again?

Long ago, people believed that eclipses were omens, foretelling sinister events to come. Today we know that eclipses are natural phenomena that occur when the sun, moon, and Earth are aligned. Click on the links at the above Web site to learn more. Then figure out which set-up below causes a solar eclipse and which one a lunar eclipse. Label and caption the drawings, explaining how the eclipse occurs.

_____ **Eclipse**

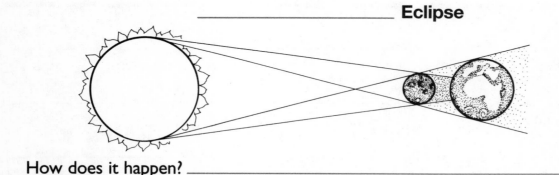

How does it happen? _____

_____

_____ **Eclipse**

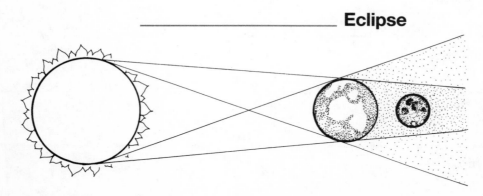

How does it happen? _____

_____

Name: _____ Date: _____

GO TO: http://www.scholastic.com/profbooks/easyinternet/index.htm

Eclipses

Solar Eclipse in Jeopardy

Think you have all the answers when it comes to solar eclipses? What about the questions? Click on the links at the above Web site to read more about solar eclipses. Look at the answers we've provided below. Then write the correct question for each answer. Make sure your question is related to solar eclipse.

1. Q. _____
   A. Umbra

2. Q. _____
   A. Penumbra

3. Q. _____
   A. Annular eclipse

4. Q. _____
   A. Bailey's beads

5. Q. _____
   A. "Diamond ring" effect

6. Q. _____
   A. Nodes

7. Q. _____
   A. Total eclipse

8. Q. _____
   A. Path of totality

Name: _____ Date: _____

GO TO: http://www.scholastic.com/profbooks/easyinternet/index.htm

Auroras

Sky Lights

You're standing in the cold, dark night staring up at the stars when suddenly you see a colorful curtain of light form and ripple through the sky—an aurora! Explore the links at the above Web site to view and read about auroras. Then answer the questions below.

1. What two places on Earth are you most likely to see auroras?_____

2. What out-of-this-world event causes auroras to appear on Earth? _____

3. How high up in the sky do auroras begin? _____

4. In which part of the Earth's atmosphere do auroras occur? _____

5. What is solar wind? _____

6. What is the magnetosphere? _____

7. What two factors determine the color of an aurora? _____

8. What gas causes the rare red aurora and at what height? _____

9. What do you call an aurora at the north pole? At the south pole? _____

_____

10. How are the Earth's geographic poles different from its magnetic poles? _____

_____

Name: _____ Date: _____

GO TO: http://www.scholastic.com/profbooks/easyinternet/index.htm

Auroras

What Causes Auroras?

People who live near the Earth's poles have the fortune of being able to see auroras in their night skies. But what causes these spectacular sights? Click on the links at the above Web site to find out what causes auroras. Then number the steps below in the order in which they happen.

_____ Energy-packed solar wind slams into the Earth's magnetosphere (magnetic field), compressing it.

_____ A stream of light—an aurora—appears in the Earth's upper atmosphere.

_____ Solar wind carrying electrically charged particles from the sun bursts at high speeds out into space.

_____ Electrically charged particles collide with gas atoms in the Earth's ionosphere, the upper layer of the atmosphere.

_____ Charged particles travel along the Earth's magnetic field toward the magnetic north and south poles.

_____ Gas atoms in the ionosphere absorb excessive energy, causing them to release light and other electrons.

Trivia Tracker The sun goes through a predictable cycle of increased solar activity before it quiets down again. Auroras on Earth become more intense as the sun's activity increases. How often does this increased solar activity occur? _____

Name: _____ Date: _____

GO TO: http://www.scholastic.com/profbooks/easyinternet/index.htm

Space Exploration

Space Pioneers

When the space race began in the 1950s, many dreamed of being the first person to reach space. Explore the links at the above Web site to learn about the men and women who made space history. Write two or three sentences about these astronauts' contributions to the space race.

Alan B. Shepard, Jr. _____

_____

John Glenn, Jr. _____

_____

Neil Armstrong _____

_____

Guion S. Bluford _____

_____

Sally Ride _____

_____

Eileen Collins _____

_____

Name: _____ Date: _____

Space Exploration

Extraterrestrial Explorers

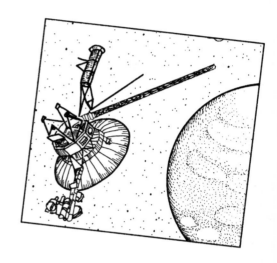

Eager to learn about our otherworldly neighbors, we've sent probes to explore the planets in our solar system. Click on the links at the above Web site to find out more about these space explorers. Then fill in the chart below.

Spacecraft	Planet Destination	Arrival Date/Year	Amazing Facts
Viking			
Magellan			
Voyager			
Galileo			
Cassini			

Name: _____ Date: _____

Space Exploration

Weigh Off in Space!

Astronauts who walked on the moon discovered that they were much lighter there than on Earth. Find out what you would weigh on other planets (and the size of each planet) by clicking on the links at the above Web site. Then fill in the chart below.

Think About It!

Is there a relationship between your weight on a planet and the planet's mass or size? What is it?

Planets	Planet's Mass	Planet's Diameter	Your Weight
Mercury			
Venus			
Earth			
Mars			
Jupiter			
Saturn			
Uranus			
Neptune			
Pluto			

Name: _____ Date: _____

GO TO: http://www.scholastic.com/profbooks/easyinternet/index.htm

The Periodic Table

Find the Missing Elements

The periodic table is an ingenious way of organizing all the known elements. Click on the links at the above Web site to study the periodic table. Find the symbol for each of the elements below, then write the symbol in the correct space in the periodic table.

1																	He 2
Li 3	Be 4											B 5	N 6	7	F 8	9	10
11	12											Al 13	P 14	S 15	Cl 16	17	Ar 18
K 19	Ca 20	Sc 21	Ti 22	V 23	Cr 24	Mn 25	26	Co 27	Ni 28	29	Zn 30	Ga 31	Ge 32	As 33	Se 34	Br 35	36
Rb 37	Sr 38	39	Zr 40	Nb 41	Mo 42	Tc 43	Ru 44	Rh 45	Pd 46	Ag 47	Cd 48	In 49	Sn 50	Sb 51	Te 52	53	Xe 54
Cs 55	Ba 56	La 57	Hf 72	Ta 73	W 74	Re 75	Os 76	Ir 77	Pt 78	79	Hg 80	Tl 81	82	Bi 83	Po 84	At 85	Rn 86
Fr 87	Ra 88	Ac 89	Rf 104	Db 105	Sg 106	Bh 107	Hs 108	Mt 109	Uun 110								

Ce 58	Pr 59	Nd 60	Pm 61	Sm 62	Eu 63	Gd 64	Tb 65	Dy 66	Ho 67	Er 68	Tm 69	Ub 70	Lu 71
Th 90	Pa 91	92	Np 93	Pu 94	Am 95	Cm 96	Bk 97	Cf 98	Es 99	Fm 100	Md 101	No 102	Lx 103

1. Hydrogen _____   6. Yttrium _____   11. Copper _____

2. Neon _____   7. Uranium _____   12. Magnesium _____

3. Sodium _____   8. Iron _____   13. Oxygen _____

4. Krypton _____   9. Carbon _____   14. Iodine _____

5. Gold _____   10. Lead _____   15. Silicon _____

Name: _____ Date: _____

GO TO: http://www.scholastic.com/profbooks/easyinternet/index.htm

The Periodic Table

Element-ary Word Search

Read through the links at the above Web site to familiarize yourself with some of the words related to the periodic table. Solve the clues below, then find the answers in the word search grid. Words can be forward, backward, up, down, or diagonal.

```
A  H  Y  T  L  A  T  E  M  I  L  A  K  L  A
O  P  E  R  I  O  D  I  C  T  A  B  L  E  N
C  A  R  L  V  E  N  R  T  N  T  A  O  M  D
Z  B  I  A  E  A  R  E  G  R  O  U  P  S  J
N  I  R  L  S  C  O  B  A  C  M  C  U  I  O
S  G  S  V  A  U  T  E  Y  A  I  E  B  O  G
H  I  E  O  L  I  H  R  I  U  C  O  J  F  N
E  R  N  G  T  O  S  H  O  A  N  H  L  E  O
L  S  A  Y  C  O  L  A  E  N  U  A  N  V  T
L  U  H  S  A  A  P  S  R  I  M  R  E  S  O
L  T  N  E  M  E  L  E  D  O  B  N  U  E  R
E  A  R  N  N  R  A  T  T  A  E  I  T  R  P
C  I  N  E  R  T  G  A  S  S  R  C  R  A  R
M  R  E  Z  G  O  N  C  K  O  A  T  O  N  E
P  E  R  S  O  T  S  F  M  U  G  C  N  A  J
```

Clues:

1. The basic building block of matter
2. Substance that has only one kind of atom in it
3. Chart that lists all the elements in order of increasing atomic number
4. Positively charged particle in an atom
5. Negatively charged particle in an atom
6. Neutrally charged particle in an atom
7. Space around the center of an atom where electrons spin
8. The number of protons in an atom
9. Family of elements that includes lithium, sodium, and potassium
10. Family of elements that includes helium, neon, and argon

Name: _____ Date: _____

GO TO: http://www.scholastic.com/profbooks/easyinternet/index.htm

Energy

Build Your Energy Vocabulary

It's hard to imagine what our world would be like without energy. But what exactly is energy? Visit the links at the above Web site to learn more about energy and other words related to it. Then write the definitions of the words below.

1. energy _____

2. kinetic energy _____

3. potential energy _____

4. electricity _____

5. Btu (British thermal unit) _____

6. joules _____

7. battery _____

8. turbine _____

9. generator _____

10. transformer _____

Name: _____ Date: _____

GO TO: http://www.scholastic.com/profbooks/easyinternet/index.htm

Energy

Renewable vs. Nonrenewable Energy

Many of our energy sources are nonrenewable—they'll run out someday. We do have renewable energy sources, but they're harder to use. Read about both types of energy at the links at the above Web site. Then fill in the Venn diagram below to compare them. Fill in the middle area with things that both types of energy have in common.

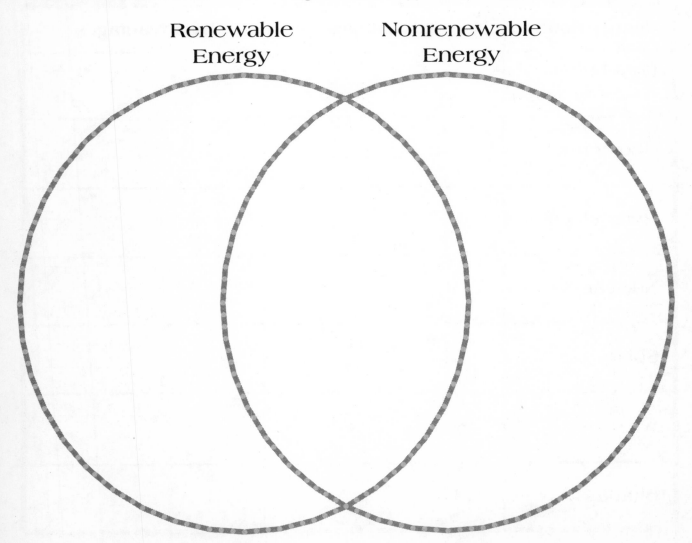

Name: _____ Date: _____

GO TO: http://www.scholastic.com/profbooks/easyinternet/index.htm

Energy

Where Does Energy Come From?

Learn about the different energy sources available to us by clicking on the links at the above Web site. Then fill in the chart below by writing the advantages and disadvantages of using each energy source.

Energy Source	Advantages	Disadvantages
Fossil Fuels (coal, oil, natural gas)		
Geothermal		
Hydroelectric		
Nuclear		
Solar		
Wind		
Biomass		

Name: _____   Date: _____

GO TO: http://www.scholastic.com/profbooks/easyinternet/index.htm

Roller Coaster Physics

The Science of Roller Coasters

Every year, amusement parks around the country try to build faster, taller, more thrilling rides. But building roller coasters requires a lot of science know-how. To learn more about the science behind these scream machines, click on the links at the above Web site. Check out the glossary for terms and definitions, then answer these questions.

1. A roller-coaster car is pulled by a chain to the top of a hill at the beginning of the ride. What kind of energy is present at this point? _____

2. What force brings the roller coaster down the hill? _____

3. What kind of energy keeps the roller coaster moving after it goes down that first hill? _____

4. In a roller coaster, which hill is always the highest— the first, middle, or last? Why do you think that is? _____

5. True or false? An object is accelerating when it is slowing down. _____

6. What's the best shape for a loop—a circle or a teardrop shape? Why do you think that is? _____

7. What force is present when a roller coaster is moving through a loop? _____

8. What force slows down a roller coaster and eventually brings it to a stop? What helps bring about this force? _____

Trivia Tracker Where and when was the earliest roller coaster-type ride built?

Name: _____

Date: _____

GO TO: http://www.scholastic.com/profbooks/easyinternet/index.htm

Roller Coaster Physics

Name That Force

Think you know everything there is to know about roller coasters? Label the different parts of the roller coaster below with the different forces and types of energy that are present.

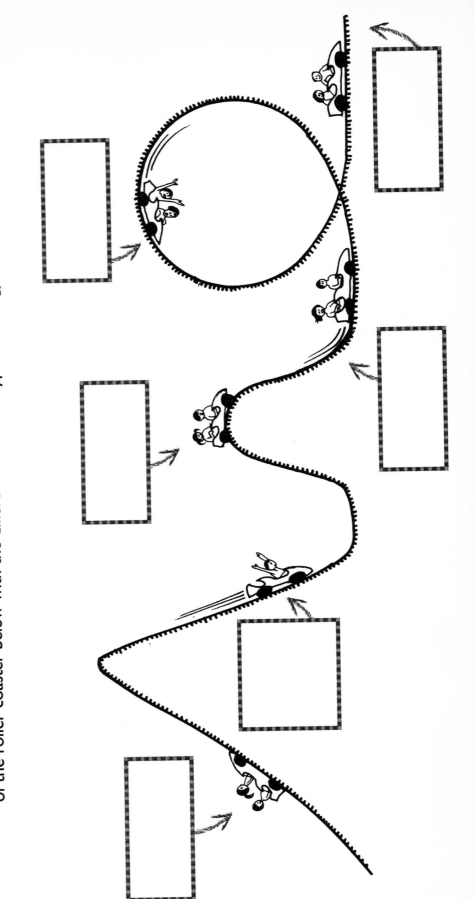